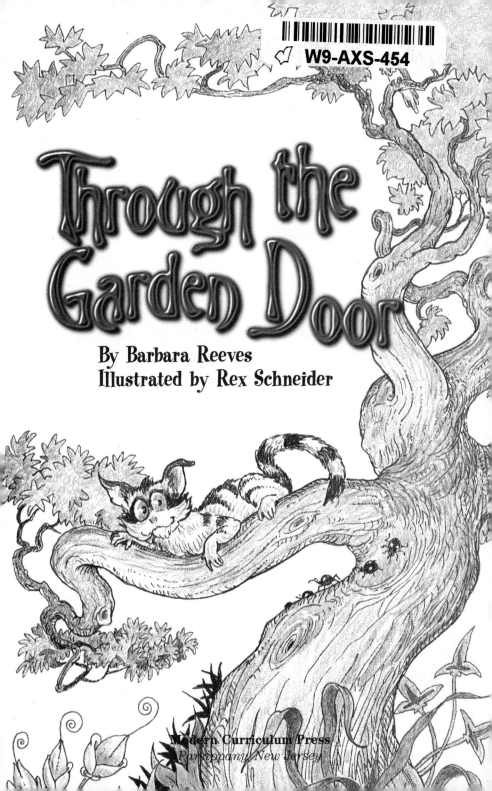

Through the Garden Door

By Barbara Reeves
Illustrated by Rex Schneider

Modern Curriculum Press
Parsippany, New Jersey

Cover Illustration: Jeannie Winston

Interior Illustrations: Rex Schneider

Cover and book design by Liz Kril

Modern Curriculum Press
An imprint of Pearson Learning
299 Jefferson Road, P.O. Box 480
Parsippany, NJ 07054–0480

www.pearsonlearning.com

1-800-321-3106

ISBN 0-7652-0895-4

6 7 8 9 10 11 12 13   MA   07 06 05 04 03 02 01

Contents

Chapter 1
The Chase Begins

When winter came, the snow started to fall. Day after day, icy winds blew and the snow came down. It piled up along the streets in dirty heaps.

Miko and Jason liked the snow at first. It was exciting to see the city covered in a frosty white blanket. But soon the snow made the city look messy. Jason and Miko soon became tired of snow.

After school one day, Jason and Miko were hurrying along the sidewalk in the dim light of the cold, gray afternoon. They were wet and chilly.

"Do you know where I'd like to be right now?" asked Jason. "I'd like to be on a spaceship." He climbed on top of a snow pile. "I'd head for a faraway planet where it never snows."

"Well, you're on Earth," said Miko. "And it snows a lot in our part of the country. So let's go home. I'm cold."

Jason jumped down. He threw a fistful of snow at Miko. She ducked as it flew over her head, spraying her with sugary snow. She looked up and laughed.

"We're in for at least two more months of winter, Jason," she yelled. "Get used to it!"

Miko expected Jason to growl and chase her with another handful of snow. But he didn't answer. He was staring over Miko's shoulder at something behind her.

"Jason, what's going on? What do you see?" asked Miko. She turned and looked.

"I think it's a cat," Jason said, pointing to a fuzzy shape ahead of them. "Or maybe it's a monkey."

"Oh, sure!" said Miko, peering ahead and trying to see what Jason was pointing to.

"No, look, Miko. It's right over there. It's not like any other cat I've ever seen. So you tell me what it is."

Miko looked across the street. Something furry was moving along the wall of the building. She couldn't see the animal clearly. It just looked fuzzy, and it had a long, striped tail.

"What . . . ?" Miko began.

Jason motioned for Miko to follow. Very slowly, he moved toward the creature.

"Jason, be careful," Miko whispered. "We don't know what it is. It might be dangerous." Jason kept moving.

"It's probably just a cat," Miko thought. She was curious to find out, too.

Café
Ladida

ONE WAY

When they got within a few feet of
the animal, it froze in its tracks. It looked
up at them with huge eyes. It was like no animal
they knew.

"Maybe it's lost," said Miko.

"Yeah," said Jason. "It probably escaped from the
zoo. Maybe it's someone's exotic pet that got loose
somehow. It looks cold and scared."

Suddenly the animal turned. It started moving quickly down the sidewalk.

"Let's follow it!" said Jason. "Maybe we can catch it. We can put an ad in the paper. There might even be a reward!"

"Forget the reward," said Miko. "The poor thing needs help. It will freeze in this weather."

They dashed down the street after the animal. They speeded up as they saw it turn the corner.

The animal slowed as it
came near a plain metal door
set in the side of a big brick
office building. The door was
open a crack. A thin stream
of light came from the opening. Without
stopping, the animal rushed up to the
door and slipped through. With a flick of
its tail, it was gone!

Chapter 2
The Open Door

Miko and Jason ran to the door and stopped. "That's funny," said Jason. "That door is never open."

"Should we go in?" Miko asked Jason.

Jason looked at the door nervously and almost said no. Then he grinned.

"Let's go!" said Jason and he began to open the door.

As Jason opened the door, a bright light flooded the sidewalk. It was so bright, he couldn't see.

"Wow!" he said.

"What is it?" asked Miko. She followed him through the opening.

As they stood together, the door closed behind them with a loud clank. In front of them was an amazing sight.

They were in a beautiful garden. The air felt
soft and warm. A light breeze tickled their
noses. The ground under their feet was springy
like a thick carpet. Bright flowers grew
everywhere. They were odd shapes and strange
colors. Bees hummed busily around many of
the flowers. Birds were singing in the trees.

Jason gave a low whistle. "There's no snow
here," he said.

"Where are we?" Miko asked in a whisper.

"I have no idea," said Jason. "But I know this is not an ordinary garden."

Miko reached down to touch a pink flower. The flower moved, brushing against Miko's hand.

"Please, don't," said a low voice.

Miko and Jason jumped, as Miko pulled her hand back. From behind a tree, a woman appeared. She was wearing green gardening overalls with a light green T-shirt. Her gray hair was tucked beneath a straw hat. She held a gardening spade in her hand. String trailed from another pocket. She didn't look happy.

Chapter 3
The Gardener

"I'm sorry," said Miko. "I wasn't going to pick the flower."

"How did you get here?" demanded the woman in a strong voice.

"We got here through, through . . ." stammered Jason. He pointed behind him toward the door.

"There was an animal," blurted Miko. "We followed it through the door. We were only trying to help."

The woman looked up into a huge tree next to her. There on the bottom branch sat the very same animal they had chased. It peered down at them.

"Chitt. Chitt. Cheee!" it cried.

"Silly thing," said the woman. "Get down from there! Look at the trouble you've started."

"Chitt. Chitt. Cheee!" the animal scolded. Its tail waved back and forth, but it made no move to come down.

"He's very curious," said the woman. "He must have found a way to get the door open and run out. There would be trouble if he hadn't come back."

"Chitt. Chitt. Chitt," chattered the animal. Then, amazingly, the tree branch on which it sat began to move downward. It lowered the animal to the ground.

"That tree branch moved!" gasped Jason. The woman only smiled.

The animal ran toward the woman and wrapped itself around her leg. Then it climbed up her overalls until it finally perched on her shoulder. It peered out from under the brim of her hat.

"There are many unusual things in this garden," said the woman. She almost smiled as the little animal brushed her ear with the long fingers of one paw.

"What kind of animal is it?" asked Miko as she looked at the furry creature.

"It's called a chatter-chee," said the woman. "Its name is Tris. This is the only place where you'll find one. It's been around here for a very, very long time. So have all the other creatures in the garden."

"Could I pet it?" Miko asked hopefully. She reached out with one hand. The chatter-chee called "chitt, chitt" more loudly.

"I don't think you should right now. Tris has never seen strange humans before. Until now, he's known only me," the woman said.

Disappointed, Miko put her hand down. "Your garden is beautiful," she said, looking around.

"Oh, but it's not my garden," said the woman. "I'm only the caretaker. I'm called the Gardener. It's my job to protect the garden, and I have been doing so for a very long time. Longer than you can even imagine. This is a secret place that no one from the outside world knows about."

The woman looked serious again. "Until now, that is," she said, frowning. "That's why you shouldn't be here!"

"Please don't be angry," said Jason. "Let us look around, just for a few minutes. It's so warm and bright here, and so cold and gray out there. We promise not to hurt anything." Miko nodded her head to show she agreed.

The Gardener looked at the children for a long time. Then she let out a big sigh. "Now that you're here, I guess I could let you stay for a few minutes. But you must promise never to tell anyone else about this place or to take anything out with you," she said, still looking at them. "If you did, the garden would die and be gone forever."

"We promise! We won't tell anyone!" cried Miko.

"Well . . ." said the Gardener. She seemed to relax. Miko and Jason hoped that she had seen they were honest, caring, and careful children. "I guess it wouldn't hurt to show you around a bit."

Chapter 4

The Garden

The Gardener began to walk down
one of the garden paths. Miko and
Jason followed. As they walked, the
children felt warmer.

Bugs that looked like jewels flew
down and landed on the children's
shoulders. Birds sang in clear, bright
voices. Each plant, tree, and animal
seemed to have a personality.

The Gardener led the children around a curve in the path until they came to a big grassy area. They saw a herd of deerlike animals.

The animals all raised their heads when they saw Miko and Jason. They didn't seem to be afraid. In fact, one of the animals came up to Miko. It nuzzled her hand and made a purring sound.

"Oh!" said Miko. "I could stay here forever!"

Suddenly, the Gardener became alarmed. "I'm afraid you can't stay," she gasped. "In fact, you have to leave now. You've seen enough."

She quickly turned and hurried the children back down the path toward the door.

"Please," said Jason as he hurried along, "can we come back again?"

"We could help with the gardening . . ." suggested Miko.

The Gardener didn't answer. She rushed them
right up to the door and put her hand on it, as if to
open it. Then she stopped and looked into the
children's eyes. Her face began to soften.

"It might be nice to have company once in a
while," she said. "I live in a world that time has
forgotten. I get lonely. I shouldn't do this, but
something tells me I can trust you two."

"Oh, yes, you can trust us," said Miko.

"Come back tomorrow, then," said the Gardener. "Knock on the door three times. Wait exactly one minute. Then knock three more times. I'll let you in. Until then, the garden is off-limits. And don't forget. Tell no one where you have been. Goodbye."

The Gardener opened the door and almost pushed the children out. The cold air greeted them in a rush. They quickly finished putting on their coats and mittens.

"What a strange woman," said Miko.

"What a strange place!" said Jason. "I can't wait until tomorrow!"

Chapter 5
Back to the Garden

The next day went slowly for Miko and Jason. It was hard not to talk about the garden. But they kept quiet, even when Kim, a curious classmate, asked them why they were smiling.

"I don't see what you two have to smile about," Kim said in a grumpy tone. "It's snowing again."

"We try not to pay any attention," Miko said.

"That's impossible!" grumbled Kim.

Miko didn't reply. She hurried away with Jason before Kim could say any more.

After school, the children hurried down the street. They looked behind them many times to make sure that no one was following them. Then they rushed back to the metal door.

They knocked three times. Then they waited exactly one minute, as the Gardener had told them to do. They knocked three more times. Then the door creaked open.

The Gardener pulled them in quickly, shutting the door tightly behind them. She greeted them with a smile.

"So you came back!" she said. "I thought you would. Now follow me!"

Warmed by the air, the children quickly took off their coats and left them near the door. They followed the Gardener down a garden path. Miko breathed in deeply.

"The air smells wonderful," she said.

"The flowers in the garden give off a delicious smell," said the Gardener. "And they're special in another way. Watch."

The Gardener reached into her pocket. She took out a handful of flat purple seeds. She bent down and scratched a hole in the soft dirt with a garden tool. She put the seeds in the hole and stood back.

Miko and Jason couldn't imagine what was going to happen next. Then Jason looked at the sky. He pointed up. "Look!" he said to Miko.

A small fluffy cloud was floating down toward them. It moved lower. Then it settled over the spot where the seeds were planted.

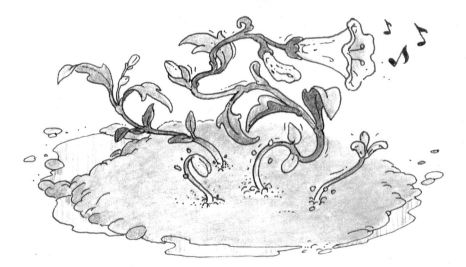

The cloud turned gray. Then rain streamed
from it onto the ground. The children watched
the ground closely. Suddenly the seeds began to
sprout. Green shoots rose up. The cloud floated
away as quickly as it had appeared.

The green shoots grew into a small plant.
Buds formed on the plant within seconds. Then
they opened into yellow trumpet-shaped flowers.

"How beautiful!" said Miko. She pushed her
nose into one of the flowers and took a sniff.

"Lemon drops!" she cried. "The flowers smell
like lemon drops."

"Listen," said the Gardener. She snapped her
fingers twice, and music filled the air.

"You see," said the Gardener, "in this garden,
trumpet flowers really do make music. Now
follow me. There's more!"

As the children followed the Gardener, they discovered other delights. They found flowers that smelled like cinnamon cookies and strawberries. They heard the insects hum songs. They watched animals play in grass as green as emeralds.

Time passed quickly. What seemed like minutes turned into an hour as the children continued to explore. They had never seen plants and animals quite like what they saw in the garden.

Finally, the Gardener pulled out a pocket watch. It played a few notes of music.

"Garden time," she explained. "And it looks as if it's time for you to go. Remember to keep the garden a secret."

Again, the children promised the Gardener that they would tell no one. Again, the Gardener looked at them seriously.

"I trust you to be careful," the Gardener said. "But I must also warn you. Sometimes, no matter how careful you are, you say or do something that gives away your secret."

As the Gardener walked the children to the door, she said, "I hope you come back again. I've enjoyed your visit. I've forgotten how wonderful it is to share this beautiful place with others."

Leaving the garden was just as much of a shock as it had been the day before. Out on the gray city street, Miko sighed. "It's so hard not to tell others about the garden," she said.

"Miko!" cried Jason. "If other people find out about the garden, they'll ruin it! And then it won't be there for us to visit, either."

"I know, I know," said Miko. "It's just that the garden seems like a dream when we're not there."

"Well, we'll go back again tomorrow," said Jason. "The garden is our own special place now. We have to protect it."

Chapter 6
The Big Mistake

Day after day that winter, the children returned to the garden. Soon, they were helping with the garden chores. They planted seeds and made sure the animals had enough to eat. They kept Tris busy, playing hide-and-seek among the trees. Then, one day, the children made a mistake.

One evening, after they left the garden, Jason said, "Let's stop at the store on our way home."

"OK," Miko replied. She reached into her shirt pocket to get a couple of quarters. Along with the quarters, out came several purple seeds.

"Oh, no!" she cried, staring at the seeds.

Jason looked at the seeds with horror. "You can't have those out here!" he yelled.

"I didn't mean to take them," said Miko. "I was going to plant them. Then Tris wanted to play. I must have put the seeds in my pocket. Then it was time to go, and I forgot they were there!"

"Are those all the seeds you have?" asked Jason. "Check your pocket again to make sure."

Miko poked around in all of her pockets. "That's it," she said.

"Let's count them," said Jason.

"Two, four, six, eight, ten," counted Miko.

Jason turned back to the door. He knocked hard three times. Then he waited one minute and knocked again. The Gardener did not come to the door. He tried knocking again, then waited, but it was no use.

"We'll bring them back to the garden tomorrow," said Miko.

"I guess that's all we can do," Jason sighed. "But I have a bad feeling about this. The Gardener was so serious about our not taking anything from the garden."

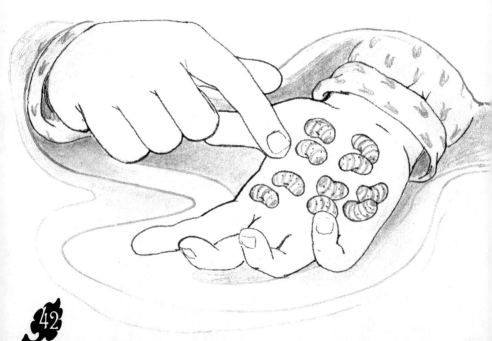

At home that night, Miko found a small
box and carefully put the seeds inside. She
counted them from one to ten as she placed
each one in the box. Then she put the box
under her pillow.

The next morning she carefully put the box
in her book bag. When she was sure no one
was looking, she checked the box and
counted the seeds again and again.

After school, Jason and Miko quickly walked to
the corner. Then Jason asked about the seeds.

"I have them right here," said Miko. She
unzipped her book bag and pointed to the box.

"Let me see them," Jason said.

"Two, four, six, eight, ten," she counted as she
placed them in Jason's hand. She had to stand
close because of the cold wind.

"Good. They're all here," he sighed. Then he
put them back in the box. "Let's go!"

They knocked on the garden door, hunching
their shoulders against the cold. Once inside, they
told the Gardener what had happened.

"Where are the seeds now?" she asked. Her
face lost its smile and now looked worried.

"Right here," said Miko. She opened the box.
"Two, four, six, eight, nine . . ." she counted.
"Oh, no! There's one missing!"

The Gardener's face turned pale. "You must
find it," she gasped. "Go back, quickly!"

Chapter 7
The Search

The children rushed back outside. They began to search the street where they had walked.

"Where do you think we dropped it?" asked Miko. "It's so small, I'm afraid we'll never find it!"

"It could be anywhere," Jason said. His eyes swept back and forth over the sidewalk, looking for anything that might be a purple seed.

"Wait a minute!" Miko stopped. "What about the place where we opened the box and counted them? Maybe that's where we dropped it."

The children began to run. They hurried around the corner and down the next street.

"Over there!" Miko pointed. They rushed to the spot.

"Look!" shouted Jason.

A light shone from a grate in the sidewalk. The children ran over and looked down. They saw a small plant struggling to grow. The plant glowed faintly.

"That's it!" cried Miko. "We must have dropped one of the seeds through the grate when we were counting them. The plant is already growing. It's trying to get out."

"We have to act fast," said Jason. "I don't think the plant will last very long in this cold."

Jason got down on his knees and reached down into the grate. His fingers just managed to touch the plant. He grabbed the stem as firmly as he could. Then he tugged gently. At first, the plant didn't move. Jason tugged again.

"Come on, little plant," Jason said. "I'm not going to hurt you."

The light from the plant glowed a little stronger. Jason gave one more tug, and the plant came loose. He carefully pulled it from the grate.

"Let's get back to the garden!" said Miko.

Then she heard a voice behind her.

"Miko! Jason! What are you doing?" Miko turned to see curious Kim standing a few feet away.

"What did you just take out of the grate? Let me see!" she demanded. She walked toward them. Before Jason could hide the plant, Kim saw it.

"What kind of plant is that?" she asked. "I've never seen one like it. It's glowing."

"Oh, Kim . . . hello," Jason said. He whirled around, turning his back to Kim.

"Oh, no," Miko moaned to herself. It was not a good time for Kim to show up.

Miko smiled weakly at Kim.

"I think it's a weed," she said. "We were just pulling it out of the grate."

"A weed growing in the middle of winter?" asked Kim. "That seems pretty strange."

"Well, stranger things have happened," said Miko.

"Why are you trying to hide it if it's just an old weed?" Kim said. She looked suspicious. "Let me see it!" she shouted.

"I don't think so," said Miko.

"Time to get going," Jason said loudly. "See you in class tomorrow, Kim!" Miko and Jason began to back down the sidewalk.

"Wait!" called Kim. But by this time, Jason and Miko had run down the street.

They headed toward the garden as fast as they could. But before they got to the door, Miko turned around. Kim was running after them!

"Keep going!" Miko yelled at Jason.

Jason dashed by the door. It was open a crack. Miko yanked the door shut as she ran by.

They ran around the block and ducked into
a doorway. They pressed themselves into the
shadows, hoping Kim wouldn't see them.

Luckily, Kim ran on by, looking everywhere. They
leaned out and watched her run down the street.

"Now!" Miko hissed. They ran from the doorway
and back down the street the way they had come.

As they reached the door, the Gardener opened it.
She looked as pale as Miko and Jason did. Just as
they went through the door, they heard a voice yell
"Hey!" in the distance. They didn't stop.

The children gasped as they stepped inside the garden. They couldn't believe how faded all the colors appeared. The garden was beginning to die. "What have we done?" moaned Miko.

Chapter 8
Saving the Garden

The children couldn't believe what they saw.
The garden had changed completely.

"Did you find the seed?" the Gardener gasped.

"Yes, it had started to grow," Jason held up
the plant. It, too, was beginning to wilt and fade.
"But what happened?" Jason asked.

"There's no time to talk," the Gardener
panted. "Quickly! Put the plant in the ground
NOW!"

Jason used his hands to scratch a deep hole in
the soft dirt. Miko pushed the plant in the hole.

They held their breath and watched the
drooping plant, hoping it was not too late.
Then they saw the leaves lift a little.

Suddenly, before their eyes, the garden came
back to life. The sky brightened. Birds began
singing. Tris came out from behind a tree. The
Gardener's cheeks turned pink again.

"You came just in time," sighed the Gardener.
"After you left, the garden began to die. It was the
missing plant, you see. When it started to grow
outside, the garden changed. If you hadn't brought
it back, everything would have disappeared."

Miko and Jason were shocked. They knew the garden had to be protected. But they didn't think one missing plant would destroy it.

"I took a chance letting you into the garden," said the Gardener. "You made a mistake. That happens with people from the outside world. But you were quick to fix what went wrong. I'm grateful for that."

Miko looked around the garden. It seemed even more beautiful than before. She thought about the lost seed. She thought about their close call with Kim.

Miko loved the garden. Jason did too. But Miko knew the garden was more important than their feelings.

"We have to stop visiting the garden," Miko said. She tried to blink away the tears in her eyes. Jason hung his head and nodded.

"You're very wise children," the Gardener said. "I will miss you, but you must not come here again. That one mistake almost destroyed this beautiful place. Maybe you can return someday. Until then, I have to make sure that the garden is protected. From now on, the door will be locked."

The Gardener walked the children to the door. The children felt sadder than they had ever felt in their lives. But they knew they were doing the right thing.

"We'll never forget you," said Miko.

"And we'll always keep the garden a secret," added Jason.

"Thank you," said the Gardener. "I hope your lives are filled with flowers and happiness."

Out in the cold again, the children heard the door lock behind them.

Later that month the sun began to warm the city streets. Spring was finally coming to the outside world. But Miko and Jason felt as cold as the winter. Even worse, they had to walk by the secret door each day. It reminded them of what they had lost.

Then one day the door was gone. New bricks blocked the space where it had been.

"We'll never see the garden again," moaned Miko.

"Don't worry," Jason said. "I think if the Gardener wants us back, she'll let us in."

"I miss the trees," said Miko. "I miss the plants. I want to smell flowers again and watch animals play."

Jason pointed to a park across the street. Tulips and daffodils shone in the sun. Squirrels played in the trees. The grass was beginning to turn green.

"Come on," Jason said. He pulled Miko toward the crosswalk. "We have a new garden to explore," he said. "And while we're there, we can pretend that we're visitors from Mars!"

"Jason," Miko laughed, "being friends with you is always an adventure!"

Glossary

curious (KYOOR ee us) wanting very much to know something

exotic (eg ZAHT ihk) strange and different

grate (grayt) a metal frame with bars set in the street to cover a water drain

mistake (mih STAYK) an act that is wrong; an error

ordinary (ORD ih nair ee) usual, common; not special in any way

personality (pur suh NAL uh tee) the special qualities that make a person different from another person

promise (PRAHM ihs) an agreement to do or not to do something

protect (proh TEKT) to guard or defend against harm or danger

shock (shahk) to upset the mind or feelings with sudden force

suspicious (suh SPISH us) thinking or feeling that something is wrong